Flamingos!

Fun Facts and Photos about Flamingos for Kids

Joanna Slodownik

While every precaution has been taken in the preparation of this book, the publisher assumes no responsibility for errors or omissions, or for damages resulting from the use of the information contained herein.
FLAMINGOS! FUN FACTS AND PHOTOS ABOUT FLAMINGOS FOR KIDS
First edition. March 1, 2023.
This Amazing World Press
Copyright © 2023 Joanna Slodownik.
Photos: Pixabay, Wikipedia Commons

What's inside

- Fun Facts about Flamingos............................... 3
- Physical characteristics of flamingos 6
- Why are flamingos pink?.................................. 6
- Flamingos can fly! 18
- How do birds fly? 18
- Flamingos can run on water! 19
- Why do flamingos have such a long neck? 22
- Flamingos beaks are amazing......................... 24
- Why does a flamingo stand on one foot? 22
- Flamingos build their nests from mud! 29
- Are flamingos smart? 32
- Where do famingos live?................................. 34
- Flamingos are descendants of dinosaurs!........ 36
- Are flamingos endangered?............................. 35
- How do flamingos communicate? 39
- Read More Books 40

Fun Facts about Flamingos

Have you ever seen a bird that stands tall as if on stilts, with a long neck like a snake and feathers as pink as bubble gum? If you have, then you've met a flamingo!

Flamingos are truly amazing creatures. They're not your everyday backyard birds—these tall, elegant waders can be found in far-off places like Africa, Central and South America, and even parts of Europe and Asia.

There are six different species of flamingos in the world, namely greater, Chilean, lesser, Andean, puna or James's, and American or Caribbean. From the greater flamingo (the tallest of them all!) to the lesser flamingo (the smallest but still impressive), each kind has its unique features. But no matter which type you see, you'll always spot their trademark long legs, curvy necks, and of course, those fabulous pink feathers!

The greater flamingo can stand as tall as 4.7 feet! That's taller than many kids. And when they spread their wings? Wow! Some flamingos have wingspans that stretch up to 5 feet across. These beautiful birds love to hang out near water, but they also can spend a lot of time on land. You'll find them splashing about in lakes, lagoons, and mudflats. They're not fans of the deep ocean—they prefer shallow waters where they can wade and hunt for their favorite snacks.

Now, you may wonder: what makes a flamingo a flamingo? Well, like all birds, they're warm-blooded, lay eggs, and have beaks and feathers. But flamingos are special. They are so distinct, it's impossible to confuse them with any other animal.

Why are flamingos pink? How do they eat upside down? And what's the deal with those long necks? Keep reading, to uncover all these secrets and more about these fantastic flamingos!

As birds, flamingos are warm blooded, lay eggs, and have beaks and feathers.

Flamingos are water wading birds typically living near lakes, lagoons, and mudflats.

Why are flamingos' feathers pink?

When you think of the flamingo, you think of an elegant, vibrantly colored bird, usually poised on one leg. They almost look a little like goofy pink, giraffe-like swans. But where do they get those gorgeous pink and red colored feathers? Is it genetic?

Not at all! Flamingos aren't born with those vibrant colors; they are born with gray feathers; and not all adult flamingos are pink.

So, if the color is not hereditary, where does it come from?

You know the saying: you are what you eat?

It's 100% true for flamingos!

Flamingos get their pink color from their diet. They eat lots of tiny shrimp and algae, which have a natural pink dye called carotenoids.

And the more shrimp and algae they eat, the pinker they get!

***Carotenoids** give carrots their orange color or turn ripe tomatoes red. Human skin, too, if we consume a lot of carotenes, abundant in foods such as the carrots, can turn slightly orange. But flamingos don't eat carrots or tomatoes. Flamingos consume carotenoid-rich algae, larvae, and brine shrimp.*

Flamingos have waterproof feathers!

How do flamingos stay dry while splashing in water? They naturally produce special waterproof oil, which they rub all over their feathers with their beaks—it's called preening. When flamingos are preening, they are grooming their feathers and applying the oil. This oil keeps their feathers neat, shiny, and waterproof, helping flamingos to stay buoyant in the water. Another amazing thing that helps flamingos in the water is their webbed feet.

Do flamingos have ears?

You may wonder–where are flamingos' ears? Like all birds, flamingos don't have external ears. The ears are just openings into the ear canal and are protected by a covering of feathers.

How long do flamingos live?

Flamingos live 25 to 30 years in the wild, and have been known to live up to 50 years in captivity.

Do flamingos' knees bend backwards?

A common belief is that the knees of a flamingo bend "backward." On the first glance, that's what it seems like, but it's not actually what happens. It's not flamingo's KNEE joint bending backward, it's the ANKLE!

The knee is located further up the leg, very close to the body, hidden under the feathers. When the leg bends, it's actually the ankle you see hinging, and the joint that looks like an ankle, right down the bottom, is the beginnings of the toes. So effectively half the flamingo's legs are their feet, which means flamingos stand and walk on their TIPTOES!

Birds who look like flamingos

There are several birds similar to flamingos, but birders who pay attention to the details will never be confused about who they see. Check the next pages and identify who is who.

Spoonbills: Some spoonbills, such as the roseate spoonbill, are pink, just like flamingos. But their bill is much longer with a flattened, scoop-like tip. Plus, spoonbills are shorter than flamingos, and their necks are thicker.

Herons: Large herons and egrets are wading birds like flamingos, but their feathers are not pink. Plus, their beaks are straight and they hunt by stabbing at their prey instead of filtering through the water like flamingos do.

Ibises are not pink, though the scarlet ibis can be a bright red and may appear pink if its diet does not contain enough pigments to colorize its plumage. Ibises are much smaller than flamingos, with shorter legs, and thinner and longer bills.

Storks are wading birds, and some storks even have some pink feathers, but they are not as pink as flamingos. A stork's bill is longer and heavier than a flamingo's, and most storks are white and black.

Cranes can be as tall as flamingos, and they have thin legs and necks. But crane's beaks are smaller, and although they are wading birds, they so nor live exclusively near water like flamingos are.

Flamingos are not:

Swans

Cranes

Red ibis

Heron

8

Spoonbills

Flamingos are not:

Flamingos are not naturally pink from birth. Flamingos' color varies depending on what they eat.

Carotenoids give carrots their orange color and turn tomatoes red when they are ripe. But flamingos don't eat tomatoes or carrots. Carotenoids are also found in the microscopic algae that brine shrimp eat. As flamingos dine on algae and brine shrimp, their body metabolizes the pigments — turning their feathers pink.

What makes flamingos pink?

Flamingos are filter feeders!

Flamingos are filter feeders, meaning they use their beaks to strain out algae and small crustaceans from water. When a flamingo spots something yummy—a shrimp, a snail, or some plantlike water organisms called algae—they plunge their head into the water, twist it, and scoop the food using their upper beak like a shovel, pushing the water out.

Other animals who are filter feeders are whales and oysters! Of course, whales and oysters don't have such cool beaks.

Image by: Valdiney Pimenta CC BY 2.0

The name flamingo comes from Portuguese or Spanish flamengo, meaning "flame-colored". The name of the genus, Phoenicopterus, in Greek means 'crimson or red-feathered'. A group of flamingos is called a "flamboyance."

Flamingos' superpowers

Flamingos live in harsh environments, where other animals cannot survive. Imagine a lake so salty that if you swam in it, it would make your skin sting! These lakes are called soda lakes or salty lagoons. Flamingos have filters in their beaks that let them drink salty water. These filters remove the salt, making the water safe to drink. So, while other animals might not survive in such salty and hot places, flamingos thrive there, standing tall and pink!

There is so much salt in these lakes it can burn the skin. How is that for some amazing superpowers?

Are these flamingos awake or asleep?

Flamingos can sleep with one eye open

Flamingos and other birds can sleep with one eye open. While sleeping with one eye open, one hemisphere of the bird's brain is awake while the other is sleeping. The awake half allows them to watch out for potential dangers and predators.

Flamingos can fly!

You may think–duh, of course, they can; they are birds! But that is not so obvious, since there are many flightless birds, meaning they can't fly. Examples include penguins and ostriches, kiwi and the dodo. Kiwi are flightless birds living in New Zealand. The dodo is an extinct flightless bird that inhabited the island of Mauritius, which is east of Madagascar in the Indian Ocean. Chickens and turkeys also can't fly very far, if at all. But flamingos are great at flying and can travel long distances when migrating from one place to another and back.

How do birds fly?

Flight is birds' most important adaptation to their environment. It allows them to reach places inaccessible to most other animals. Birds make flying look so easy; they just take off and fly. But flying is one of the most complex forms of movement in the animal kingdom. Every aspect of flying–taking off, hovering, and landing–is incredibly complicated. Over millions of years of evolution, different bird species have adapted to their unique environments, developing their wings and flight in unique ways.

> There are various theories on how bird flight evolved, including flight from falling or gliding (downward tree hypothesis), running and jumping (upward ground hypothesis), or wing-assisted running on an incline.

Birds fly by flapping their wings and steering with their tails. Their feathers are light and the shape of their wings is perfect for lifting their bodies off the ground. Besides wings and feathers, birds have other physical characteristics that work together to enable them to fly. They have lightweight, hollow bones, which reduces the body weight. They don't have heavy teeth or jawbones, and have beaks instead. Their large chest muscles allow them to move their wings. Plus, birds lay eggs because they couldn't fly with the weight of their babies inside of them.

Birds have well-developed brains and keen eyesight, so they can react quickly to what is happening. When approaching a tree or cliff, a bird has only a few seconds to choose a spot for landing and avoid crashing. Birds' eyes are much larger in relation to their body size than humans' eyes, and most birds have much better eyesight than humans.

Flamingos can "run" on water!

Considering their height, long legs and neck, it's hard to imagine a flamingo can actually take off. But they can! They need to gather speed before taking flight. A flamingo will begin takeoff by running at full speed and rapidly flapping their wings.

Flamingos are able to "run" on water, thanks to their webbed feet, to gain speed before lifting up into the sky.

Once in the air, flamingos fly with their head and neck stretched out in front and their legs trailing behind, maximizing their aerodynamic efficiency and conserving energy by soaring.

Flamingos are migratory birds

With wingspans of 37 to 65 inches, and weighing just about 2-6 pounds (1-3 kilograms), flamingos can fly long distances. Their migrations are usually short distance in search for new food sources or to avoid a disturbance of their current habitat. Some flamingos will travel to breed, migrate to a new body of water as seasons change, or move to warmer, lower-altitude areas for the winter. If flamingos are traveling long distances, they usually travel by night.

With wingspans of 37 to 65 inches, and weighing just about 2-6 pounds (1-3 kilograms), flamingos can fly long distances.

Do flamingos migrate?

Flamingos are short-distance migratory birds. They travel mostly to find new food sources or to avoid the disturbance of their current habitat.

Image by MarioM CC BY 2.5

22

Why do flamingos have such a long neck?

Flamingos are famous for their beauty and unique style, but why do they need such a long neck? Flamingos use their long neck to find and reach for food in the water that they would not be able reach otherwise due to their long legs. They eat aquatic plants, small fish, mollusks, and other invertebrates. Their necks are amazingly flexible, allowing them to move their head freely in all directions, even turning it 180 degrees or more. Thanks to their necks, they can forage under water, in the mud and shallows on the water's edge, and on land.

Although giraffe's neck can be eight feet long, it only has 7 neck vertebrae, the same number as humans! However, unlike human or swan's neck bones, each of theirs can be up to 10 inches long.

Flamingos' beaks are amazing!

Flamingos use their curved beaks to filter food from the water. They can submerge their head underwater to move the bottom with their beak and get food.

They can hold their breath under water for several minutes as they search for delicious things to eat.

Flamingos' throat, on the other hand, can take on hot water from geysers and saltwater, which they filter if no fresh water is available.

You may have seen what look like teeth lining the edges of flamingos' beaks and mistaken them for teeth.

But, like all birds, flamingos don't have teeth. Instead, they have hard structures called lamellae around the edges of their bills.

Do flamingos sleep standing up?

Flamingos can sleep standing on one leg, sitting or drifting on water. Like many other birds, flamingos are perfectly content sleeping on just one leg. How is that for a comfortable sleeping position?

Why does a flamingo stand on one foot?

You will often see flamingos standing on just one leg—it's a wonder they don't tip over. They can stand on one foot for long periods of time—even long enough to fall asleep. But why do they choose such an uncomfortable position? And don't they ever fall down?

First of all, remember that flamingos live on caustic salt flats, where there's often nowhere to sit or lie down.

Plus, this pose helps conserve body heat in cold water.

Some birds stand on one leg to control their body temperature during cold weather by keeping more heat close to the body the same way people put hands in their pockets when it's cold. Herons, geese, hawks, and gulls often maintain a one-legged stance while keeping the other leg tucked up into their body feathers for warmth. And for extra comfort, they tuck their bill into their feathers as well. This helps them do two things. First, it warms the bird's bill. And, second, these birds can breathe in warmer air.

And if you think that this is tiring for flamingos—it's not. The one-legged stance is a very stable position, which helps save energy. In fact, flamingos use more muscle power when standing on two legs.

This is an unusual but very stable position, with the foot directly beneath the bird at the precise angle that triggers the joint lock that stops the bird from toppling over while sleeping.

It's all about gravity. The flamingo's center of mass is in just the right place, in front of its knee, and the knee itself can only move in a limited way. So when the foot is placed at just the right angle, the flamingo's weight is all that's needed to lock the joints in their leg, thus making it possible for even a sleeping flamingo to stand on one leg for hours on end.

28

Flamingos build their nests from mud!

A flamingo's nest looks like a mini mud volcano, with room for one or two large eggs. Both mom and dad build the nest and incubate the egg. Flamingo chicks hatch with delicate white-gray feathers and straight bills, and only after several years their acquire their pink color and hook-shaped bills.

Parents can easily recognize their chicks by their appearance and the sounds they make. This is important because flamingos do not feed the chicks of other birds. The young leave the nest after about a week when they are strong enough to move stably on their own. The young group with other chicks and form a "nursery" where parents find them at feeding times.

Photo Credit: Tobin Müller
CC BY SA 3.0 via
Wikimedia Commons

Flamingo parents feed their chicks a liquid they secrete, called 'crop milk'

A flamingo's "milk" is produced in their crop (part of the throat) and then brought up through the mouth. It may sound icky, but just like mammal's milk, a flamingo's crop milk is chock-full of healthy nutrients with plenty of proteins and fats. Both parents produce crop milk to feed their babies until they are old enough to eat on their own.

Flamingos are social!

Flamingos are known for being extremely social creatures. These flamboyant birds are almost always found in flocks in the wild. And during breeding season, they can gather by the hundreds and even thousands. Like all animals, flamingos cherish their families and value their own lives. Their social nature means that they're always looking out for their families and other members of their group.

In their natural habitat, flamingos spend hours wading and searching for food. They also love relaxing and napping while standing on one leg, preening their feathers, stretching their wings and flying, sleeping and snuggling together, mating and taking care of their young. They are outgoing, social animals who feel most at ease when they're in large groups, called colonies or flamboyances.

Are flamingos smart?

Compared to whom? Humans? Other birds or animals?

Comparing flamingos to humans, or even to chickens, crows, or parrots, makes little sense. Just as comparing pigs to dogs (or children), cows to horses, dolphins to fish is like comparing, well, apples to oranges. Animals develop incredible specializations depending on the environment they live in, and making comparisons between species is rarely meaningful.

Flamingos evolved to live in one environment, pigeons, crows, ducks, eagles, penguins and parrots in another, and fish, elephants, zebras, monkeys and humans still in another. So far you have learned about some amazing flamingos' superpowers, but what do the experts say?

Studies have shown that birds are self-aware and can distinguish themselves from others. They learn from one another, such as a baby learning from their parents which foods are good to eat and where to find them. Birds can also show complex problem-solving skills.

Pigeons can be taught to distinguish between the paintings of Picasso and Monet. Ravens can recognize themselves in a mirror. And crows have been spotted to leave walnuts in a crosswalk and let passing traffic crack them. Many bird species are incredibly smart, yet among humans the "bird brain" often doesn't get much respect.

Birds can complete complex mental tasks, learn from watching each other, demonstrate self-control, and worry about the future. They comprehend cause-and-effect relationships and understand that objects still exist even after they're hidden from view. They are very intelligent animals.

Can flamingos swim?

Because flamingos have such long legs, they can wade into much deeper water than most other birds, plus their webbed feet support them on soft mud. But are they good swimmers? When the water is beyond their wading depth, flamingos swim at the surface while feeding.

What is home to flamingos?

Flamingos thrive in harsh environments. Their preferred habitat is saltwater or brackish waters (where saltwater and freshwater mix). But some flamingos breed and raise their young in extremely salty bodies of water, called alkaline or "soda" lakes, hyper-saline lagoons, or high-altitude salt flats.

There is so much salt in some of these lakes it can burn the skin, making the environment uninhabitable for most animals.

These conditions are perfect for flamingos because they can find lots of algae and small crustaceans to eat and breed.

When there's no access to freshwater, flamingos can drink water from hot springs and geysers. They remove excess salt from the water using special glands in their head to make it safe for consumption.

Flamingos developed these capabilities over the course of evolution, as they have adapted to living in highly toxic settings.

One such place is Africa's Great Rift Valley. The microscopic blue-green algae called cyanobacteria that can be found there produces poisonous chemicals capable of fatally damaging most animals' cells, liver, and nervous system. Amazingly, flamingos can consume many of the algae with no ill side effects.

Lake Natron in Tanzania and the toxic Lake Bogoria in Kenya can strip the human skin bare, and many animals perish in these toxic salty waters. But flamingos thrive in these places, thanks to their tough skin and scaled parts of the legs and feet that prevent them from getting burned.

These toxic conditions have one important advantage—they provide a safe haven from predators. This allows flamingos to raise their offspring in mud nests surrounded by a caustic moat.

Flamingos thrive in extreme environments, such as highly salty waters at high altitudes, where few animals can survive.

Flamingos are living descendants of dinosaurs!

That's right! Those sweet, colorful, graceful and slightly goofy birds are close living relative to the T-Rex. Scientists have proven the shared common ancestry between birds and the *Tyrannosaurus rex*. The truth is, all birds that walk, swim or fly across our planet are technically dinosaurs, descended from giant creatures in the same family as Tyrannosaurus Rex.

If you enjoyed the Jurassic Park movie and wished you could see those reptiles for yourself— you can! There are real dinosaurs just outside your window, only we call them birds. Birds belong to the theropod group of dinosaurs that included *T. rex*. *Archaeopteryx*, discovered in 1861, is considered a transitional species closest to the origin of birds. These creatures lived during the Late Jurassic era (about 150 million years ago). Other dinosaurs closely related to birds, like *Velociraptor*, can be from the Late Cretaceous (100- 66 million years ago). Not all of the dinosaurian close relatives of birds could fly.

A feathered dinosaur is any species of dinosaur with feathers. It's possible that many, if not all non-avian dinosaur species also had feathers. Feathers' original function may had been thermal insulation, before their modification in birds into structures that support flight.

Since scientific research began on dinosaurs in the early 1800s, they were believed to be closely related to modern reptiles, such as lizards. The word 'dinosaur,' first used in 1842 by paleontologist Richard Owen, comes from the Greek for '**terrible lizard**'. Later on researchers found evidence that dinosaurs were much more closely related to birds, which descended directly from the theropod group of dinosaurs.

Illustration depicting an individual of Acheroraptor with pennaceous feathers

So what do you think? Is there family likeness?

Image by: Emily Willoughby, CC BY SA 3.0

Flamingos are a keystone species!

Flamingos play a vital role in their environment. They are known as a **"keystone species"** because they help support the entire ecosystem where they live. Flamingos' activities, like stirring up mud with their feet and filtering water for food, create healthy wetland habitats. These actions make it easier for other animals to find food and shelter in the same area, making the wetland a better place for lots of different creatures to thrive. Without flamingos, many other plants and animals in the wetland would be in trouble. So, keeping flamingos safe helps protect many other species, too!

Are flamingos endangered?

Most flamingo species are not endangered, although the Andean flamingo is listed as vulnerable, and the Chilean, lesser, and Puna flamingos are near threatened. Human activity hurts flamingos, for example, some lakes in the high Andes were regularly visited by flamingos but because of human disturbance, they can't live there anymore. In Bolivia's salt flats, colored lagoons and flamingo sanctuaries attract thousands of visitors each year. Both climate change and tourists are endangering the country's flora and fauna.

Has climate change affected flamingos?

Knowing how resilient flamingos are, one might think that nothing can hurt these birds. But climate change is altering the water table and foraging areas, impacting flamingos' access to food and their ability to breed, threatening their future. Global warming can dry out the lagoons, lakes, and swampy areas where flamingos live.

Flamingos mostly use their voices to communicate. They'll make loud honking noises during the flight, like geese. On land, the sounds they make are quieter.

How do flamingos communicate?

Flamingos communicate in complex ways, with each sound having a specific meaning, much like their own language. By making distinct sounds for different reasons, they can pass a variety of messages to other flamingos, including warnings of danger, mating calls, stress signals, food discovery, or simply letting others know how they are feeling.

How are flamingos similar to people?

Just like humans, flamingos are capable of feeling a whole range of emotions that are similar to what we feel in similar situations: joy, fear, pain, boredom, fondness, curiosity, aversion, stress, worry, and love. In many respects, flamingos are very much just like us.

So what is your favorite thing about flamingos?

Quiz Time!

Reading fun facts is addictive. We hope you had as much fun reading them as we had compiling them! Here is a short quiz to see how much you know about the elephants. Answers can be found below (but don't peek before answering!).

1. Where can flamingos be found?
A) Only in Africa B) Only in South America C) Africa, South America, Europe, and Asia D) Only in Asia

2. How many species of flamingos are there worldwide?
A) Four B) Six C) Eight D) Ten

3. What is the tallest species of flamingo? A) Lesser flamingo B) Andean flamingo C) Greater flamingo D) American flamingo

4. Why do flamingos have pink feathers? A) It is genetic B) From eating foods rich in beta carotene C) They are born with pink feathers D) From sunlight exposure

5. What do flamingos eat?
A) Fish B) Algae, larvae, and brine shrimp C) Leaves D) Small birds

6. What kind of feet do flamingos have? A) Clawed feet B) Hoofed feet C) Webbed feet D) None of the above

7. How long do flamingos usually live in the wild?
A) Up to 20 years B) 25 to 30 years C) 50 years D) 75 years

8. Which part of the flamingo's body bends, giving the illusion of backward-bending knees?
A) The knee B) The ankle C) The hip D) The neck

9. Why do flamingos stand on one leg? A) To rest
B) To conserve body heat
C) Because they can only lift one leg
D) To attract mates

10. Why do flamingos make special oil?
A) To make their feathers pink
B) To waterproof their feathers
C) To attract mates
D) To help them fly better

11. Do flamingos have ears? Where are they? A) On the top of their heads B) They don't have ears
C) Underneath their feathers
D) On the side of their heads

12. What food makes flamingos pink? A) Red berries B) Pink flowers
C) Carotenoid-rich algae and shrimp
D) Pink fish

13. What is a group of flamingos called? A) A flock B) A herd
C) A pack D) A flamboyance

14. What habitat do flamingos need to survive?
A) Deep ocean waters
B) Shallow brackish waters
C) Tall grasses D) Dry deserts

15. What do flamingo chicks eat?
A) Plants B) Insects C) Crop milk produced by parents D) Small fish

40

Read More Books

Thank you for reading! If you enjoyed it, check out more books about birds and other amazing creatures by Joanna Slodownik. And don't forget to leave a glowing review on the bookseller's page.

To find more books and download a free ebook as a gift to you, go to: JoannaSlodownik/kids.

Quiz Answers: 1C, 2B, 3C, 4B, 5B, 6C, 7B, 8B, 9B, 10B, 11C, 12C, 13D, 14B, 15C.

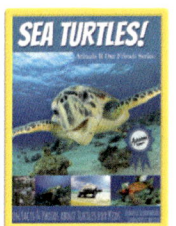

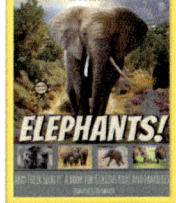

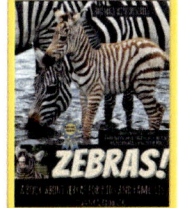

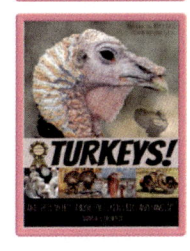